TO DROWN AS A CURE FOR THIRST

POEMS | BLAKE AUDEN

central
avenue
PUBLISHING

2022

Published by Central Avenue Publishing, an imprint of Central Avenue Marketing Ltd.
www.centralavenuepublishing.com

TO DROWN AS A CURE FOR THIRST

Trade Paper: 978-1-77168-278-7
Ebook: 978-1-77168-279-4

Published in Canada
Printed in United States of America

1. POETRY / Subjects & Themes - Love   2. POETRY / Grief

1 3 5 7 9 10 8 6 4 2

I think this one
is for me.

CONTENTS

3

TO DROWN AS A CURE FOR THIRST

1

TELL ME SOMETHING GOOD

and let it build
a home inside us.

tell me when god
opens a window
we're not on the thirteenth floor.

that your hands
on my shoulder

are really wings,
and it's not the falling
that kills us.

tell me the building
isn't burning,

that we can turn our backs
and the glow
is really daybreak.

tell me the night
is simply our shadow, leaving.

that the glinting steel
is not a blade,

but only a portion of day,

beckoning us
to follow.

A LOOP

the memory
replaced with hunger.
the hunger replaced with weight
and then, remembering.

suppose tomorrow
is just yesterday
       moving.

suppose distance
is really measured
       in time

and you are always
a little further
       away.

the memory
replaced with darkness.
the darkness replaced with yellow
and then, remembering.

I HAVE CARVED YOUR NAME INTO MY BREASTPLATE

the train
rattles the windows
and the pressing dark
between my vertebrae.

what have we done
to each other?

you, now a shadow
stitched to my neck,
arterial rust blooming
beneath my skin.

i am sorry
for not being braver,

but i can
never love you
in the way
you want me to.

WE DON'T LET GO

because this version
of the story
is the one
we can't accept.

but these are
the only bodies
we have.

all that remains of the book
is a sentence.
all that remains of the sentence
is a word.

close your eyes
and name it night.
touch my skin

and we'll call it forgiveness.

I HAVEN'T GRIEVED

because you were

        never really

        leaving,

    just gone.

this broken skin

        an answer

        to the grinding question

    of morning.

EXIT WOUND

this is how
we love each other:

powder-burnt skin,
and your throat
a barrel,

every word
an exit wound
down my spine.

and how
i will think of you:

a fire,
masquerading
as light;

a wound,
still holding
a promise

of healing.

STATIC

the voice is not my own
and so, i listen,

static turning
and breaking into poems.

or, not poems,
but a kind of heaving,

and the shameful rhythm
i find in loss.

she is the softest
of today's miracles,

drying wood
burnt and yet

not lost
between the flames.

HEAVY LIGHT

perhaps, this is the quietest
of the ways i ache

here, above the crumbling
persistence of water.

see, i am still trying
to dig them out of me,

all the coiled words
and restless moments

we let burrow into our skin
                    and grow.

but you cannot bury
darkness with light.

what i mean is,
hope is a fleeting thing,

and everything bright
can't help but leave

a shadow.

TIME, RUNNING

the sky, sealed
with orange, folds across
the distant hills,

just an exhale of light
from darkness.
   yet, i am holding
   my breath.

look down, instead,
and pretend we can stop
the day from leaving;

pretend we can bury
the rivers
   and hold them, still,
   from moving.

WYE

the river

    cuts through the green

      like a word

          and i, too,

            can move only

               in one direction.

LET ME SHOW YOU WHAT I KNOW ABOUT TIME

i.

i swear there are
parts of me that haven't

finished dying,

and to hurt
is only an act

of remembering.

ii.

they wear the same expression
in every memory i have,

which is another way of saying

that i'm starting to forget
what they look like.

iii.

the next part is softer
than i expected.

what i mean is,
depression is a skilled butcher,

every whetted edge
slipped quietly

between the ribs.

A LULLABY FOR INSOMNIA

the bulb flickers /
        once /
        and then / yields /
light /
        swallowed whole /
        by hungry / dark /
i reach /
        for something /
        in the black / air /
and find it is /
        empty /
        find only / myself /

ANOTHER SMALL WEIGHT

i have this memory
from childhood
of a couple at the wake.

he wore a gold ring,
speckled and dull,
and the backs of his fingers

were bruised
by the memory
of her cheekbone.

and she was smiling, somehow,
which is why
i remember it,

as though love
were a thing
to be beaten into.

i'm still
not sure why
i carry them.

another small weight
i don't know how
to put down.

BECAUSE YOU LOVED HER

you drive to a city
that has long since forgotten you,
the roads lit yellow
and scarred with night.

the same night
that spit you into morning,
because the grave is another home
that doesn't want you.

her door is the same
wind-worn blue you remember,
but you cannot bring yourself
to open it.

because the mouth
is also a crypt, and nothing here
can be resurrected.
and so you tell yourself

this will be the last time.
you tell yourself that she is better off,
and your skin bristles
only with winter.

I CAN STILL BLEED IF YOU'LL LET ME

tell me you don't know
if you can love me
and you have never thought of me
as a writer.

tell me you would
want me
if only i were
a little less broken.

kiss me softly,
but keep your eyes open
and maybe
i can write you

        something

           to stay for.

SUNDAY, AND IT'S ALL A MATTER OF PERSPECTIVE

i'm awake early enough
to watch the sunrise,

the ground beneath me
kindled green with light.

it hasn't always
been like this,

but loving someone
is complicated.

i feel the stirring
of dead things

between the ribs
and move a little,

the ground beneath me
burnt dark with shadows.

THERE IS LITTLE POINT IN MOVING ONLY TO WELCOME STILLNESS

... but / what if we change /

our lives / still /

the people / we have always been /

bodies / wet and weighted /

with memory /

and these objects / still relics /

of a life / wasted / but ...

HOW TO CARRY SOFTNESS

i.   i can feel you
pressed softly
against my neck,

even the thought of you
remembered white
on my skin.

ii.   i speak it,
and your name
is delicate

and alive, here
in the dying curve
of my tongue.

iii.   i have never known
how to make a home
of this body,

but it carries you so easily
that perhaps it is
                yours.

THE MEMORY IS A SECOND GRAVE

you are so much more
than the story you tell yourself,

and to be haunted is a matter of choice,
a soiled relic in the crypt of your palm.

turn your head, love,
and look with me.

each ending is a beginning,
and the sun shines orange if you let it.

2

UNDER

the glass finds its way
into the muscle,
and i press down

because what else
is there to do with pain
if not encourage it?

i push deeper
to see if the bone
might feel it,

if the marrow
still holds anything
but fear.

the phone rings
and i panic
about the body

inside my own,
about all the edges lost
beneath this skin.

I'M AFRAID TO DIE

or perhaps i mean
i am trying to live
but i don't know how.

the rain on the window
adds a gentle rhythm
to the morning,

and i am thinking
of the versions of myself
i let perish

against these tiles.
but gone doesn't
always mean lost,

and i swear her reflection
is gentle
beneath my jaw.

I DON'T KNOW HOW TO CHANGE

look, i want
to be better
than this.
but self-preservation
is a single
apartment,
and anxiety has built
an entire city
beneath
my tongue.

TUESDAY, 25 MAY

and finally
i arrive at her lips,

tongue rolling the seconds
into crushed glass.

i want to hold
this moment

between my teeth
and promise not to bite down.

i want to remember you.
i want to remember anything

other than just our names turning
in closed throats.

HEARTBREAK IS HABITUAL

and again
i find myself here,
shinbones
       scraping concrete,
another name etched
into the back of my hand.

and again
the pattern shall repeat:
another woman
       i couldn't hold,
another memory
i can't let go.

THIRTY-SEVEN

the

problem

with

immortality

is

that

it's

temporary

STILL CAN'T SLEEP WITHOUT DREAMING

the daily rebirth is heavy,

haunted now
by dreams of you:

your salt-slick hands, trembling,

a leather-wrapped
shard of light

held to my neck.

A MAIORE AD MINUS

we become
only the space
left behind us,

a name
etched
into a clock tower.

i have looked
for my shadow
raked

against morning grass,
to remind myself
i am still

here.

I KNOW NOT WHAT IT IS TO FORGET

the rain
taps the window
like memory,

every leaf
bowing to acknowledge
the weight

of water.

IT SHOULDN'T FEEL LIKE WINTER

the snow began falling
                gently
around lunchtime,
and since then the ground
has been accumulating
            white
in that slow, quiet way
that nobody seems to notice.
i think the darkest parts
of anxiety
are a little like that:

                it isn't there
                and then it is.

IT IS ONLY IN LIGHT THAT WE KNOW OURSELVES

i have written about light
as though i knew it,

as though it had ever
found a way through the bone.

i have spoken,
as you might, of water,

as though it has ever
quenched the yearning of thirst.

and watch it now, spilling softly,
and think to call it a flood,

as though it ever
had the mercy to drown me.

LET IT KILL YOU

let me rest,

here,

between the parting homes

of your molars,

and trust

that you will not

close,

that the jaw

is something other

than a waiting

loss.

AN EXCHANGE OF TINY SCULPTURES

i close my mouth / to speak /
words cleaved / from muscle /
heavy / with time / and days /

watch me / unpick /
healed skin / and carve /
a story / from the darkest / bone

watch me / yield /
another piece / another memory /
until all / i am / is paper /

and ink / in the throat / of another.

PANIC, AND THEN BREATHE

the bone rattles
in the boy's hands,

left here to lever breath
from the night's mouth.

he feels most
like a man

with blood-tinted skin,
even when the red

is from his own wrists.
            call him soft.

            call him weak.
call him by its name

and they both
shall answer.

YOU, LIKE ALL OF US

are a multitude
      of dead
      and dying people,
and i can love
only one.

do you remember
the last time
you held something

other than fear
between the edges
of your fingers?

      look ahead
and the past
can't hurt us.

      look behind
and the future
won't find us.

I HAVE FORGOTTEN HOW TO DIG

what i mean by that
is, this body is covered
with shallow graves,

moments i want to forget
buried a thumb's width
beneath this skin.

some nights i wonder
if it's too late
to cut them out of me.

some nights they pull
themselves through the gaps
as i sleep.

IT'S NOT THE FALL THAT KILLS US

is this how it will always be:
our past sharpened
against your collarbone
and slipped in pieces between my ribs?

still you hold my name in your mouth.
still i wait for you to spit the bones into my hands
as you leave.

but i wait
because i love you,
and because i don't know what to do
with space between my palms.

TODAY

is one
of those days
when i am not
really here.
of course,
it looks like me:
memories pulled
into the shape
of a boy
and sealed soft
with purple.
but it is
something less,
another reflection
i don't quite
recognize.

> another moment
> that refuses
> to stay.

EVERY SURFACE HOLDS THE COLOR OF BLOOD

to bleed is simple.

the body is always ready
to open,

to yield to another
whispered edge.

the air runs black,
and i can close nothing

but my eyes.

IT IS ALWAYS THE PAST THAT HOLDS US

the sun weeps
across the newborn morning
to wake us,

both heavy
with the weight
of memory.

and what remains
of those days
behind us?

nothing
but a door
we cannot open

and another
we cannot
close.

there is so much light here,
and yet we hold
nothing   at all.

TO DROWN AS A CURE FOR THIRST

the quiet makes a home
at the nape of my neck,

only to welcome something sharp.

i swear i had a voice, once.
but it is lost to the idea

that only the first sentence really matters.

what is this silence i have become?
yet another refuge

lost to a darkening sea:

a new tremble
waking from the center of my palm.

THE ONLY GOD I KNOW IS THE THING THAT BREAKS ME

in the cathedral
of my body
i kneel,

because worship
is an act
of looking up.

and here, beneath
vaulted rib
and a beating altar,

i carve a space
for myself.
for a faith that touches

only the things that cut.
and still i hold
out my hands

and ask for forgiveness.
still they return to me
wet with blood.

WHAT OF US WILL BE LEFT, BUT OUR DOUBTS

i.   anxiety knits
line language;
      bone growing
      on top of bone.

ii.   is this the cost
of living:
each second
another ruined seed
beneath the gum?

iii.   the machinery
of heart and lung
gathers time,
adorning the skin
      like rust.

iv.   yet, they move.
still they sing
      to the cadence
      of rain.

STANDARD-BEARER

the anxiety
    is a painted flag:

        wind-torn
        and hung heavy

    from the mast
of my spine.

I CAN STILL CHOOSE TO STAY

the wind trembles
on your breath
and i swear

i can still
choose to stay.
i can still

unpick every goodbye
ferried deep
into the marrow.

for years
i was a murmur
caught in the throat,

until you taught me
to open my jaw
and sing.

ALL THAT DARK AND ALL THAT COLD

you speak
and the words crack
and splinter
beneath the weight of it:

the fear
birthed red
into the violence
of morning.

but do not
think me lost,
or another exhale
dreamed into earth.

the chest is a sky
of birds, still.
every beat your own
private murmuration.

THE END AND BEGINNING OF ALL THINGS

i watch you admire
the ochre bled into evening,

the horizon
another dying animal.

and i understand
something new about myself:

i am heavy everywhere
         except your arms.

TURNING QUIET

i enter
every second
and still
they leave.

i think
the past
is always
growing,

pulling
every still moment
beneath
the ground.

what if this
is something
i deserve?

what if
the blade needs no reason
to cut?

NOTHING NEW

to remember is to relive,
and to live is to endure.

        but you know this already.

winter has gone,
but i don't think it has forgiven me.

i'm not sure
it has forgiven you, either.

        but you know this already.

i am sure
forgetting is an act of mercy,

even when it's the only thing
you're afraid of.

PAPER TOWN

the light cuts
a blade across your body,

and i wonder
if you are still fighting the urge
to run.

i know you have built
this church before,

worshipped at an altar
now crumbled and overrun
with green.

what if i swore
to help bury your dead?

turned earth beyond the stone
with the only hands
i have?

would you love me
the way you wanted to?

would i be any harder
to mourn?

ARS POETICA

what is poetry
    if not
        the translation
    of silence?

DOLOROSA

what if the only way
　　　　　forward
　　is back?

what i mean is,
i'm scared
you're still grieving.

and what is grief
if not the persistence
of want,

the determination
　　　of love
　　　　　to stay?

TO SHED A LIMB

the strongest part
of my body

is what it carries;
like the branch

scarred with lightning,
i am defined

by the things
i have survived.

i want more
than this,

but to reach out
and touch the world

is to be changed by it,
and i am no longer

the person
i was.

THE BODY REMEMBERS

the tree fights
against the chainsaw's
chewed tongue

but falls nonetheless,

another body
to embrace the earth
before you.

perhaps there is still war inside those hands.

perhaps violence
cannot be forgotten
by skin, and bone.

TO YEARN IS TO SPEAK YOUR NAME

i have known
the weight
of your hand
against my collarbone

and the carving
of your touch
from my skin.

i have known
the hollow
of yearning,

of becoming a word
stripped of meaning
and pressed to the ground
at your feet.

STILL ALONE

to write

　　　　is to create a world

　　　　you cannot

　　put yourself inside of.

to look upon

　　　　the face of a girl

　　　　you cannot

　　make real.

REFLECTION

open your eyes
and tell me
what you see
when you look at me.

does anything remain
of the journey?

of the dying
i can't wash from my skin?

am i more
than a rib cage
opening at the end
of a bullet?

       it does not matter.

i can still taste
every body buried

in the graveyard
of my mouth.

there is desperation
rooted in my wrists,

and i am a deer
rushing endlessly

toward the snare.

i am a

tower

of birds

and they

return

and rest

only at

the sound

of your

voice

A THANK-YOU

and so you drag me
from the dark, my heels
cutting a memory
through the mud.

you speak
and find the answer
in my touch, still wet
with rain.

and this will not
be the last time
you rescue me
from the trees,

or pull wolves
from my sternum
and light the cavity
with hope.

and this will not
be the last time
i love you,
every demon kneeling

at the echo
of your call.

4:07 A.M.

don't you know?

there are things
i can only say
to you
when you're sleeping,

when the night
slips
          its fingers
around my throat.

to find yourself
in someone
is to lose it
when they're gone,

and i am lost
in the ocean
of your breathing,
in the falling

darkness
          of your chest.

PRAYER

i call to you

        and only my heartbeat answers,

    the pauses between

          each closed fist

just long enough to hold you.

let me ask:

        are we destined to be broken,

   or just

          whole enough

to surrender?

MILES TO GO BEFORE WE SLEEP

these hands that have held
so much, so many,

still rest holding nothing
but themselves.

and yours,
just as heavy, as empty,

wait for me
on the other side of this night.

but what is distance
if not time spent alone?

what is love
if not desire sharpened

against every exhale
spent apart?

THERE IS NO WAR INSIDE OF ME

i.
the memories
are thick:

cement coating
piano-wire veins.

ii.
breathing is all
i ever wanted to be.

iii.
i am a color
pressing itself
against the night's teeth,

unseen
in the absence
of light.

REDUX

the tree carves a silhouette
from the horizon,

thinning limbs
bowed with color.

and what of my own resurrection?

another breath
ground from morning,

a new season of rust
leaving into my lungs.

4

BACK TO LIFE

hold me
like a book,
opened at the spine,

and let my misery
unfurl itself
from the creases.

close me
like a heavy door,
a barrier:

refuge from the coming storm.

WAITING

i am writing to you
from the other end
of this sentence,

the ink
my only measure
of distance.

or perhaps
not writing,
but waiting

for you to reach me,
here, in the only place
i ever wanted to be.

TO THE SEA

i watch the river
pinned between
the mountains,

every movement
a rush toward change,
a journey to disappear.

i think of my mother,
arms open
to call me home.

and my father,
the weight of history
between his fingers.

because each of us
is running:
hoping to return,

        forget,

      become.

AUTUMN, AND I MISS YOU

i watch the late rain,
rattled by the wind
                and past,
and notice how
        the water
                        mimics light
            on your skin.

is my touch
            still buried
                    beneath the bones
of your wrist?
                            or just newsprint
            on your cheek?

i wonder
if i am something
        the cold
                        will shake
                from your memory,

like every fallen season
                to have opened itself
        at your feet.

POST-ARGUMENT, SEPTEMBER

the morning dances
through the tall grass
and rests, breathless,
against the tiles.

we are together
but silent,
the air punctuated with keys
and the faintest ticking of time.

and even like this,
i love you.
even in the restless quiet,
in the echo of words left unsaid.

STAY

your fingers carve
channels into my neck:

a thousand new rivers
that might leave.

but i only ever wanted
to stay.

i only ever wanted
a reason

to pitch my shadow
into the earth

and be still.

A POEM FOR MORNING

dew clings
to the day's grass,
yearning
to be taken,

to be transformed
and returned
to the vacant sea.

a breeze grips
and shakes
every edgeless blade:

a field of knives
that takes
nothing but moments,

each movement
of our hands
destined
to be forgotten.

A REASON TO INHALE

it's not too late
to dig the sand

into the shape
      of everything
we left behind.

bury every prayer
uttered into the darkness,

into the night
      that promises
to swallow.

RUIN

the sky is so bruised
i want to hold it.

i promise not everything
has to open,

even if it means
letting every wound
succumb to rust.

i think i am a ruin,
which is to say

that i never meant to be beautiful,
only to endure.

maybe tomorrow
                everything
        will be
                        better,

the way every exhale
leaves your body

with little more than a promise
        to return.

i am

a ruin,

which

is to say

that i

never

meant

to be

beautiful

DON'T FORGET ME

is this not the definition of love:

to build something
you know cannot last?

and yet we build.

we hold these blades
in our mouths,

whetted against
every forgotten word,
            every sound
cleaved with longing
                  from the air.

i want to remember

every stone
            turned
                  and taken
by the wind,

the way fire remembers
every branch
encouraged into ash.

BELIEF

we make a god
                of the things
        we love.

and you have become
the only one
        i suffer for:

another savior
to press my knees
                to the earth

        and remind me
it's not enough.

LITTLE THINGS

your fingers slip
between mine,

and i don't know
what it is
not to love you.

are you still afraid
               to hold me?

i watch your skin
catch the morning
and keep it

as though you
were always a home
for the light.

say something.

      say bravery.
            healing.

      say forgiveness.

      say anything,

just let me see
your mouth move,

and i'll pretend
the shape is my name.

AN EMPTY PLAGUE

i hope to approach
the slow death
of evening

with more
than palms
filled with want,

the day
something other
than an empty plague.

i need to believe
in something,
      anything,

other than the light
shredded between strands
of her hair.

A CONSTANT GARDENER

calloused thumbs
      parting earth
            into new wounds.

every ruined seed
          abandoned
     to the darkness.

watch it grow
     without me.
         another life

that does not
         need me:
     shade under which

i will never
     know shelter
         from the sun.

CORNWALL, 7:04 A.M.

the sun climbs
over distant hills,
cutting a sorrow's width
of warmth
across the shimmering glass.

birds skim the water
beyond the rocks,
their reflection
almost part
of themselves,

the salt
promising to hold them
if only they would
        let go
     of their movement.

OLDER

the body speaks
through impenetrable tongue:

a cracking,
      a sigh,

a death rattle.

to age is to accept
the weight of the past,

to crease a thousand new moments
      into stones

and carry the beach
inside us.

i know the pull
      of history,

dragging us
to the ground

as though our bones
are longing

to be called.

        to travel.

    to return.

THAT WHICH DOES NOT KILL YOU

i.   starless sky.

            anxiety creeping

      through my bones

            like language.

ii.   can you   pin my shifting limbs?

iii.   if only i had

            the courage

      to hammer iron

            through my wrists.

iv.   to fold my carcass

            into the freezer

      of your chest

            and rot.

PANIC ATTACK FOLLOWED BY SILENCE

a bone-caged fist.
                    every vein coiled
                            and pulled tight
        in the red
of my rib cage.

i can still
                    swallow my voice.
                            even with every letter
        clawing
against the walls of my throat.

                    the walls of my home.

        the home of my windpipe.

comfort me with silence,
                    save the exhale
                            of a restless sea,
        but do not leave me
to the thunder

        of blood.

MAUSOLEUM

we suffocate in ash,

because we are left
only with what the flames
wouldn't take.

because i can't
separate myself
from the remains of it.

is it only trauma if you visit it?

only blood if it stains your skin?

watch how i carry
the dead and decaying
parts of us.

see how the body
becomes a tomb,
the mouth a scar

we can't help but open.

PERSONAL HISTORY

there are moments
i can't bring myself

to forget,

etched in stained glass
and mounted

in every salt-weathered chapel
behind my eyes.

ask me the cost
of healing.

litter these
blackened sidewalks

with bone shards
and marionettes.

how we try to let go.
how we try to hold on

to water
with ossified hands.

i would burn
every church.

every piece of wood
and dark bone

if only i had
a map to follow,

if only i knew
how to carry

a flame.

TO
DROWN
AS
A
CURE
FOR
THIRST

NOTES

"We Don't Let Go" borrows and alters language from Ocean Vuong's poem "Odysseus Redux."

"Wye" is a reference to the River Wye in Herefordshire, England.

"I Can Still Bleed If You'll Let Me" is inspired by Keaton Henson's song "Polyhymnia."

"How to Carry Softness" "The Memory Is a Second Grave" and "A Thank-You" are for Becca.

"A Maiore Ad Minus" is Latin, roughly translated to "from the greater scale to the lesser."

"It Shouldn't Feel like Winter" is an extract from my newsletter, called *Altar To The Hunted Things*. This can be found at blakeauden.substack.com.

"All That Dark and All That Cold" is a line taken from *No Country for Old Men* by Cormac McCarthy.

"The Body Remembers" is for my father.

"Miles to Go before We Sleep" contains a nod to Robert Frost's poem "Stopping by Woods on a Snowy Evening."

"There Is No War Inside of Me" is for my family.

"Mausoleum" contains a nod to the title of William Evans's book *We Inherit What the Fires Left*.

ABOUT THE AUTHOR

Blake Auden is a poet, writer, and artist living in Brighton, UK. Blake has published four previous poetry collections: *Murmuration, Tell the Birds She's Gone, Beekeeper,* and *The Things We Leave Behind.* He is a winner of the Button Poetry 2020 Short Form Prize.

Growing up with a father in the military, Blake began reading war poetry from an early age, becoming fascinated with the ability of prose to capture both deeply traumatic and cathartic experiences. Blake's work now focuses on loss, heartbreak, and mental health.